A trail guide to walking the

DART VALLEY TRAIL

from Dartmouth to Totnes

A trail guide to walking the Dart Valley Trail:
from Dartmouth to Totnes.

Copyright © Trail Wanderer Publications 2018
www.trailwanderer.co.uk
contact@trailwanderer.co.uk

First Printed 2018
Printed ISBN 978-1-9999509-2-7

By Matthew Arnold.
Editor - Scarlett Mansfield.

This product includes mapping data licensed from Ordnance Survey with the permission of the controller of Her Majesty's Stationary Office.

© Crown copyright 2018 OS Licence number 100059542.

St George's Church, Dittisham

TABLE OF CONTENTS

How To Use This Guide	1
General Introduction	4
- What Is The Dart Valley Trail?	
Characteristics of the area	5
- The River Dart and the Dart Estuary	
Wildlife	6
- River Dart and Estuary Wildlife	
Weather	7
Preparation	8
- Accommodation	
- Food & Nutrition	
- Village Pubs, Shops and Cafes.	
Navigation	11
- Maps Covering The Route	11
- Signposts & Waymarkers	12
Kit List	13
- On Person	
- Personal Kit Carried in Pack	
- Additional Kit	
Getting to the start point (Dartmouth)	16
- By rail Then Ferry	
- By Car	
- Buses	

Leaving the finishing point (Totnes) — 18
- By Rail
- By Bus

Distance Chart — 19
- Hight Elevation Chart

The Route — 21
Leg 1 - Dartmouth to Dittisham — 22
Leg 2 - Dittisham to Tuckenhay — 30
Leg 3 - Tuckenhay To Totnes — 38
FInishing at Totnes — 42

Useful Information — 46
- Organisations
- Community Information
- Public Transportation
- Selected Eateries
- Selected Accommodation
- Taxis
- Additional Info
- Emergency Services

Notes: — 52

HOW TO USE THIS GUIDE

This guide will provide you with full instructions on walking the entire length of one of the UK's most wonderful long-distance walking paths. The following book is broken down into a number of helpful sections to provide a more enjoyable and detailed experience.

Firstly, an introductory section with background information provides a greater insight into the history and the profile of the terrain you will be traversing over. It also contains information on the abundance of wildlife that you may encounter.

Secondly, a chapter on preparation will provide all the information you need about reaching the start point, leaving the finishing point, travel information, and distances between each of the major settlements. This enables you to properly plan ahead and make your walk much more enjoyable.

Thirdly, and arguably most importantly, this section provides a detailed description of the whole route - broken down into easily manageable legs. At the beginning of each section, information is provided about accommodation, pubs, and eateries that you will encounter in that section of the walk.

Finally, at the back of the book, you will find a section containing useful information. This includes the contact details and websites of the numerous organisations, groups, and travel information bureaus you may need to ensure your trip runs smoothly.

Looking out towards the Estuary with Kingswear over to the left

GENERAL INTRODUCTION

WHAT IS THE DART VALLEY TRAIL?

With its untouched scenery, steeped wooded hillsides, and abundance of wildlife, the Dart Valley Trail is undoubtedly one of the most attractive river walks in Devon.

Around sixteen miles long, this trail takes in both sides of the valley. The eastern trail leads from Greenham to Kingswear while the western track runs between Dartmouth and Totnes. This book, however, will focus on the Dartmouth to Totnes section which covers approximately 12 miles of the trail, including a number of steep climbs.

Beginning in the historic harbour town of Dartmouth, situated at the mouth of the Dart Estuary, the town is a fantastic starting point. With its long history, charming streets, unique shops, and exceptional local produce, there is plenty to explore, see, and do.

The trail leads out of Dartmouth with an initial climb, it then proceeds up the Dart valley, weaving through varying terrain (including steep rolling hills and woodland) before passing close to the shoreline of rivers that feed the Dart. You will encounter a number of pretty, peaceful, little villages on route including Dittisham, Cornworthy, Tuckenhay, and Ashprington. In all, the route provides glimpses of breath-taking views throughout. From the high ground, you can make out the craggy outline of Haytor Rocks of Dartmoor National Park. On the other side, views stretch across over to Torbay, even as far as East Devon on a clear day in some places. The trail slowly winds to an end in Totnes, a historic market town equally steeped in history.

CHARACTERISTICS OF THE AREA

THE RIVER DART AND THE DART ESTUARY

Like many of the rivers in Devon, the River Dart begins its life high up on the Dartmoor National park as two separate tributaries, the East and West Dart rivers. The two rivers join at the appropriately named Dartmeet. The east rivers source can be found west of Whitehorse Hill while the West Dart river begins 2 km north of Rough Tor.

The name, River Dart, is believed to have derived from British Celtic meaning 'river where oak trees grow' because the banks of the lower Dart were covered in ancient oak woodland. With Dartmoor itself steeped in myths and legends, the River Dart is also subject to much folklore due to the number of lives that have been claimed over the centuries.

Due to the amount of heavy rainfall that the National Park receives, the river has a tendency to rise extremely quickly without notice. This can cause the river to become extremely dangerous as it can induce strong currents and fast rapids. Legend has it that when the swollen waters cascade down the valley and a north westerly wind blows, strange booming noises can be heard. Known as the 'Cry of the Dart' it is said to belong to the spirit of the river preparing to claim an annual life. Poet Eden Phillpots emphasises this legend, writing: "Dart, Dart, cruel Dart, every year thou claim'st a heart."

If you are up for an adventure, then Dartmeet does provide some very attractive walking routes alongside the river. This area is also extremely popular with kayakers and canoeist. Upon leaving Dartmeet, the river meanders down through the high sided Dart Valley Nature Reserve. After leaving the moor, it then flows on through the Benedictine Monastery of Buckfast Abby, as well as the towns of Buckfastleigh and Dartington before flowing on through until it meets Totnes weir, originally built in the seventeenth century. Up to this point, the Dart is fully navigable by sea. However, during spring, low tides means the river almost dries out.

It should be noted that there are no further bridges after Totnes. However, passenger ferries operate and provide transport between Dittisham and Greenway House. Two vehicle ferries also operate between Dartmouth and Kingswear. Cruises can also be taken between Dartmouth and Totnes.

Dartmouth, with its deep natural harbour, can be found towards the mouth of the estuary. Though steeped in maritime history, today commercial activity has all but declined. However, the area is still popular with local fishing vessels, private yachts, and leisure boating activities. It is also visited by the occasional large cruise ship.

WILDLIFE

RIVER DART AND ESTUARY WILDLIFE

The River Dart is much more than a river. It is an artery sustaining life as it runs its course from Dartmoor through to the estuary and on into the English Channel. If you spend some time looking into the river, you will likely be granted by many surprises.

Thankfully, due to the steep valley sides, the densely wooded slopes offer secluded stretches devoid of human development. In turn, the area offers a haven for all sorts of wildlife including a huge array of birds; you can see ospreys, egrets, gannets, buzzards, shags. Keep a look out as you may be able to spot them feeding on fish throughout the creeks along the river.

The river transforms from an upper freshwater system, with saltmarshes and reed beds, to an estuary, where a large number of marine habitats exists. The estuary has long been popular with the cultivation of shellfish – there is even a designated area at Waddeton. It is also an excellent feeding ground for a wide variety of fish including sea bass, plaice, and pollack. During the summer through to autumn, Atlantic Salmon and brown trout also begin their journey up the river to start spawning.

Finally, dolphins and basking sharks make regular visits to the coast. Porpoises are even prone to follow in front of boats that enter and leave the harbour.

WEATHER

The best time of the year to walk the Dart Valley Trail largely depends on what you hope to see and find. Wildlife flourishes at different times of the year and no single month is particularly better than another unless there is something specific you want to see.

Influenced by the North Atlantic winds, Devon generally has a mild climate. The county experiences warm summers; July and August are the hottest months to visit. The weather also starts to get warmer in May with an average high of 16 degrees and a low of 7 degrees. Summer really picks up from June to September with average highs of 20 degrees and lows on average of 11 degrees. October is somewhere between, with a high of 15 degrees and a low of 8 degrees.

When it comes to rainfall it varies across the county. In Dartmoor, the wettest months to visit are from December to March with an average of 30mm of rain every month. April, September, October, and November all average 20mm while May to August averages only 10mm. Overall, January sees the highest average of rain days with 21 days a month, while June sees the least with an average of only 13 days of rain a month

PREPARATION

ACCOMMODATION

At twelve miles long, the route is fairly short - a person of average fitness would be able to complete the route, at a brisk pace, in one day. However, if you feel like taking a more leisurely approach and taking time to explore more of the surrounding area of the Dart Valley, you will encounter a multitude of charming hotels, bed and breakfasts, and even campsites to suit all tastes and budgets.

It is impossible to give credit to all of these, however, at the beginning of each leg, you will find mentions of selected accommodation. You can find further contact information under Useful Information on page 46. Stated accommodation will normally be located close to the main trail but you should also remember to account for any added distance it may take.

It is a good idea to spend some time carrying out your own online research to find suitable stopover locations. Websites such as Booking.com and Airbnb also provide a great resource when looking for accommodation. They allow you to reserve a room in someone's home, or guesthouse, at a fraction of the cost of paying for a hotel; great if you plan on staying for only one night.

FOOD & NUTRITION

All of the settlements that you will encounter along the Dart Valley Trail are situated in close proximity. Refuelling and stocking up on supplies is therefore not going to present much of a problem. However, it is still important to plan for the entire length of your trip so that you have enough calories to sustain yourself; twelve miles is a hefty distance for most and parts of the terrain are challenging.

Ideally, you should consider each leg of your walk and think about what food you are going to need that day to help you complete the distance required. If you are going to be completely self-sufficient then this is one of the fun parts of preparing for the walk as it gives you a chance to be creative, consider what food goes well together, and perhaps even trying things you have not eaten before. You should also consider taking vitamins to supplement any lack of nutrients.

It is a good idea to separate your food into days so you know exactly what you are having on each and do not run out of food faster than expected. If you have allowed yourself extra days for a detour, be sure to account for the energy needed to complete these sections too.

It is also vital to carry enough water to last you for each section. As mentioned the route can be challenging in places so it is important to take on enough fluids in order to allow your body to maintain an optimum working temperature, as you will lose a lot of fluids from strenuous activity.

If you plan on carrying your own food then make sure you have the lowest weight possible. For example, you should dispose of all food packaging before you depart as this will also rid you of all the litter you would then have to carry around as this is just dead weight. You should also aim to pack light-weight food that is easy to prepare as it will require fewer utensils to do so. If you are worried about a lack of flavour, it may be a good idea to carry small sachets of spices to make meals more exciting.

When it comes to snacks to eat on-the-go, cereal and muesli bars are great options. It is also nice to make your own trail mix. Simply purchase a bag of your favourite nuts, seeds, chocolate chips, and dried fruit and then place them into a small bag to keep on yourself for easy access and energy along the way. All of these can also be eaten separately depending on what resources you have, or that you can find along the way. Other options include rice cakes, chocolate bars, whole-grain tortillas, energy bars, chews or gels.

Again, when it comes to main meals remember to plan in advance. You should ensure that you are taking on a good mixture of complex and simple carbohydrates. For breakfast, porridge oats and wheat flakes with a bit of powdered milk mixed separately would be an ideal option. For dinner, noodles, pasta, and rice make safe, cheap, and light options although remember that rice can take a lot longer to cook. While dehydrated meals and boil in the bags are handy, they are often expensive and use both a lot of fuel and a lot of water. Of course, do not forget to pack instant coffee sachets for a refreshing cuppa to make your walk more enjoyable!

VILLAGE PUBS, SHOPS AND CAFES.

As mentioned, you will pass through a number of settlements en route and they all offer some form of local amenities such as pubs, cafes, and village shops. You will have many to choose from. Here you can stock up on supplies, or just have a generous meal in one of the pubs. At the start of each section, a number of selected facilities will be listed. Make sure that you account for the time spent in each place as well as the opening and closing time of aforementioned establishments.

NAVIGATION

The trail is a recognised footpath so you will find it marked on OS mapping. Below, you will find a list of OS maps that you may require. The trail has its own emblem, two stylised castles, and can be seen attached to the familiar footpath sign posts. These can be found very frequently throughout and are marked in both directions.

If you do require additional maps then the scale of a map will depend on how much detail you wish to look at. Even though you can see footpaths on OS Landranger Mapping, OS Explorer maps tend to be more popular with walkers as they offer a greater detail of the terrain, therefore, I would certainly opt for the 1:25 000.

An example to offer more guidance on scale is in the following example. If you have a map at a scale of 1:25 000, every 1cm represents 25 000cm, in turn equalling to 250m in real life.

OS Explorer Maps are broken down into 4cm gird squares, with each grid square equalling 1km. OS Landranger Maps have 2cm grid squares equalling 1km.

MAPS COVERING THE ROUTE

OS Explorer Maps
1:25 000 Scale
4cm or 1 grid square = 1km

OS Explorer OL28
Dartmoor

OS Explorer OL44
Torquay & Dawlish

OS Landranger Maps
1:50 000 Scale
2cm or 1 grid square = 1km

OS Landranger 191
Okehampton & North Dartmoor

OS Landranger 202
Torbay & South Dartmoor,
Totnes & Salcombe

OS Landranger 192
Exeter & Sidmouth

SIGNPOSTS & WAYMARKERS

Below are some of the examples that you will encounter and should keep a lookout for.

KIT LIST

As with any expedition, planning is of paramount importance thus compiling a suitable kit list of needed items is an essential task. Narrowing down the items that you need will ensure that you have a happier and safer experience. Depending on the type of outing that you have in mind, whether it be a country ramble, a backpacking holiday, or scaling the largest mountain ranges in the world, you are going to have to create a kit list specific to your expedition.

As mentioned, the route from Dartmouth to Totnes is roughly 12 miles long, however, it is up to you how long you take to reach the end of your trip. You need to think about how many hours or days you will spend completing each section and prepare your kit accordingly. Below I have provided a kit list that will give you some idea of the equipment that you might want to consider. This is a standard kit list of items that I often take with me on my walks. Of course, you should tailor it to your needs.

You can print this kit list out by visiting
(www.trailwanderer.co.uk/information/kit-list.pdf).

ON PERSON

Item	Notes	✓
Walking boots		
Walking trousers		
Map & Map cover		
Notebook and pen	Keep a note of accommodation on the route.	
Watch	Smart watch to log the route	
Beanie hat		
Buff		
Compass		
£50 / Wallet	Enough cash or transport or supplies.	

PERSONAL KIT CARRIED IN PACK

Item	Notes	✓
Waterproof Liner	A waterproof liner for the inside of the pack	
Sleeping bag		
Bivvy bag		
Roll mat		
Warm kit	Softie down jacket	
Spare socks	4 Pairs	
Spare underwear	4 Pairs	
Towel	Antibacterial towel	
Jet boil / Cooking system	Spare gas	
Hoochie / Tent	Tent pegs	
Bungees	5	
Hydration pack	2 litre	
Spare water	2 litre	
First aid kit	Plasters, deep heat, anti-fungal powder	
Food / Emergency rations	Noodles, boil in the bags, trail mix, nutrition bars	
Lighter/ matches	For lighting cooker	
Gloves		
Hand wipes	Antibacterial wipes	
Survival blanket		
Rubbish bag	For food packaging/general rubbish	

ADDITIONAL KIT

Item	Notes	✓
Spare batteries	3x AAA	
Spare laces		
Flip flops / Light weight trainers		
Portable charger		
Sun glasses		
Thermal mug		
Brew kit	Coffee / Tea sachets	
Multi-tool		
Walking poles		
Head torch		

Old Mill Creek

GETTING TO THE START POINT (DARTMOUTH)

BY RAIL THEN FERRY

One of the most spectacular ways to reach Dartmouth is via the heritage Dartmouth Steam Railway. This railway runs between Paignton and Kingswear. To reach Paignton by rail initially, transfer at Newton Abbot for the twenty minute journey to Paignton.

From Paignton, it is then a trip on the steam railway passing beautiful seascapes and down through the Dart Valley. Upon reaching Kingswear, you can take a short ferry trip across the River Dart. Both the train and ferry are operated by the same company and tickets can be used for both. The train does run throughout the year but it would be worth checking the time table beforehand.

More information on timings for the train and ferry can be found at the following link: **(www.dartmouthrailriver.co.uk/tours/steam-train-and-ferry).**

BY CAR

If you are arriving by car, a better alternative might be to leave your car at one of Totnes's carparks and catch the onward X64 bus to the start point. This would enable getting away from the finishing point much easier.

If you arriving from the north, head down the M5 and merge onto the Devon Express Way. When the road splits in two, keep right and follow signs for Plymouth, A38. Continue on this road for 20 miles and take the Dart Bridge exit signposted Totnes, A384. Continue along the A384 until you arrive at the village of Cott. From the roundabout, take the first left onto the A385 and follow along all the way into Totnes via the train station.

If you are arriving from the south, continue up the A38 and take the Marley Head exit, signposted Paignton, A385. Keep to this road all the way through to the village of Cott. At the roundabout, continue straight over and continue along until you reach Totnes.

Parking can be found next to the station. Alternatively, you can find parking in the south of the town, just off St Katherines Way - a short walk from the Steam Packet Inn. Charges do apply.

More information on parking around Totnes can be found by visiting the following link **(www.visittotnes.co.uk/see-and-do/plan-your-visit/parking-in-totnes/).**

Otherwise, if you wanted to proceed onto Dartmouth, take the right before Totnes's train station onto the Western By Pass (A381). Continue along this road until you arrive at a petrol station. From here, turn left onto the A3122 and follow this road down into Dartmouth. The most convenient carpark is located to the left, just off Mayor's Avenue.

More information on parking around Dartmouth can be found by visiting the following link:
(www.discoverdartmouth.com/information-and-map/travelling-around/parking).

BUSES

If you are arriving by bus, there are two main options available. Firstly, the X64 runs between Exeter and Dartmouth via Totnes. Secondly, the number 3 route runs between Plymouth to Dartmouth via Kingsbridge. Both these services run throughout the week with a reduced service on Sundays and bank holidays.

More information on Devon bus travel routes can be found by visiting the following link:
(www.traveldevon.info/bus/interactive-bus-map/)

LEAVING THE FINISHING POINT (TOTNES)

BY RAIL

Located to the north of the town, Totnes railway station sits on the main rail line that runs through the South West and provides onwards travel to Penzance or to London and beyond to the north. The station also offers many facilities including refreshments, toilets, waiting rooms, and a ticket booth.

Trains serve the station roughly every 10 minutes; most run between Penzance and London Paddington. Connections to further destinations can be made from either Exeter or Newton Abbot.

BY BUS

If you feel that getting away would be more convenient by bus then you have the choice of the Gold route, running between Torquay and Plymouth via Totnes, or the X64, running between Dartmouth and Exeter via Tones. Both provide locations that offer connections to onwards travel. These services run throughout the week with a reduced service on Sundays and Bank Holidays. A number of smaller routes also operate around the surrounding area.

DISTANCE CHART

Dart Valley Trail	Km	Miles	Elevation Gain
Dartmouth to Dittisham	6.9	4.2	358
Dittisham to Tuckenhay	6.6	4.1	180
Tuckenhay to Totnes	6.1	3.7	186
Total	**19.6 km**	**12.1m**	**723 m**

The mileage chart, pictured above, is useful to indicate the distance between each of the major settlements on route. As well as this, the chart also shows the expected elevation gain within each leg of the walk.

You can see from the chart below, the route contains some very steep ascents and declines, which begin as soon as you leave Dartmouth. The ascents can be challenging in places.

HIGHT ELEVATION CHART

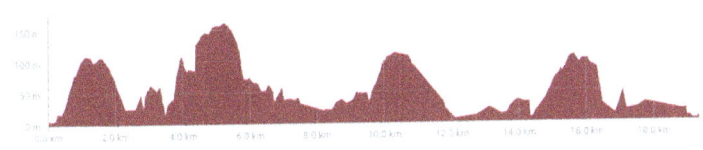

Please note: All figures given are approximations, these distances and elevation will vary based on diversions.

Trail leading through Great Copse

THE ROUTE

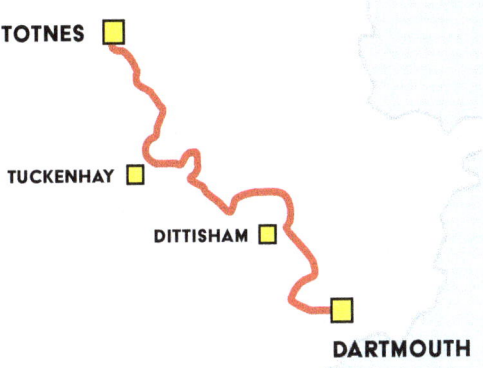

LEG 1 - DARTMOUTH TO DITTISHAM

Dartmouth Harbour

Dartmouth

OS Grid Ref: SX 879 514
District: South Hams
OS Explorer map: OL20 South Devon

Leg Distance: 6.2 km / 4.2 miles
Elevation Gain: 358 m

Points of interest

Britannia Royal Naval College
Dartmouth Castle
Bayards Cove Fort
RNLI Visitors Centre
Dartmouth Harbour
Royal Adventure Gardens
Dartmouth Museum
Public Car Parking
Public Toilets

Accommodation & Eateries

Dartmouth Arms
Beth's Bistro
George & Dragon
The Floating Bridge
The Ship in Dock Inn
Wheelhouse
Café Alf Resco
Rockfish Takeaway
The Cherub Inn
Royal Castle Hotel
Browns Hotel

Buses

X64 - Exeter to Dartmouth
3 - Plymouth to Dartmouth

Dartmouth lies on the western shore of the Dart estuary. Popular with tourist, it is located within the South Devon area known as the South Hams district, a recognised 'Area of Outstanding Natural Beauty'. The area has a rich history and its presence can be traced back to the Domesday Book of 1086; a settlement, known as Dunestal, constituted the local parish.

The area has been of strategic importance for centuries. Owing to the deep water of the port, notable naval activities occurred here. In 1147 and 1190 vast fleets assembled here as it was used as a sailing point for the crusades. During the reign of Edward III, Dartmouth even became home to the Royal Navy. Further, during the hundred years war, the French sacked the port twice . To this day, it remains a home for the Royal Navy. The Britannia Royal Naval College provides initial officer training here, and it has done so since 1863.

Dartmouth Castle

Occupying a rocky outcrop, this three-storey artillery fort overlooks the Dart Estuary. The castle was ultimately built to engage enemy ships in order to protect trading and fishing in Dartmouth's harbour from the threat of a French attack. The earliest parts of the keep dates back to the 1380s while the gun tower dates back to the end of the fifteenth century. The chapel of Saint Petroc can also be found within the castle walls.

The castle remained in use for centuries; additional defensive protection was later added to circumvent the threat of attack by land. New artillery was also upgraded during the eighteenth century. A new gun position, called the Grand Battery, was added too. By the twentieth century though, the castle served its final use in World War Two. It was finally retired from service in 1955.

Today, the castle is manged by English Heritage; it attracts tens of thousands of visitors a year and is well worth a visit.

Due to the popularity of Dartmouth, and the amount of history associated with the town, you will find a multitude of facilities and charming little shops located around the harbour. From cafes and restaurants to B&Bs, all budgets are catered for.

The Information Centre provides the start point for this trail. It can be found by heading along The Quay, a few metres on from Dartmouth's small harbour. It is also located next to the main public car park.

Clarence Hill, leading out of Dartmouth

To start the trail, lead off left from the visitors centre towards the George & Dragon pub. Proceed along Zion Place and keep the George & Dragon on your right.

At the very end of the road, to the right of the garage, you will find a narrow set of steps leading up to Clarence Hill. Once at the top of the steps you will be presented with the first strenuous leg of the route, an 800 meter climb out of Dartmouth. At the top of the steps, turn left and proceed up Clarence Hill. Continue straight as you merge onto Townstal Hill and then onto Mount Boone.

At the crossroads, continue straight uphill onto Church Road. The path eventually curves around to the right, passing St Clement's Church on your left. Here, you will be please to know, the terrain levels out. You will now be located at the junction of College Way (A379) which leads down into Dartmouth. A gated entrance to the Britannia Royal Naval College is located on the opposite side, over to your right.

From the junction, turn left then take the immediate right onto Old Mill Lane and follow the road around to the left onto Townstal Crescent.

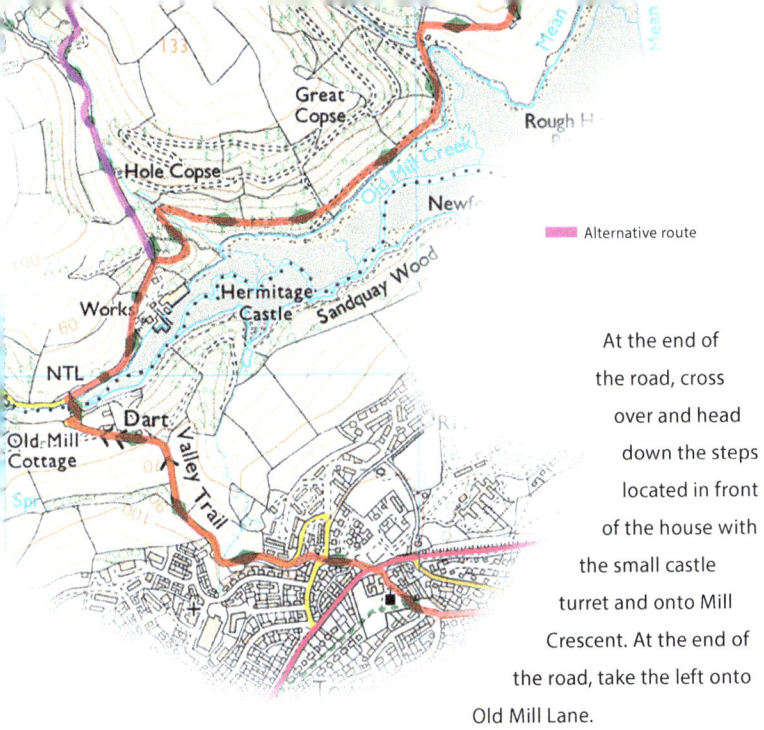

Alternative route

At the end of the road, cross over and head down the steps located in front of the house with the small castle turret and onto Mill Crescent. At the end of the road, take the left onto Old Mill Lane.

Follow the road as it leads down to Old Mill Cottage next to a picturesque stone bridge that crosses the inlet at its narrowest point. The bridge provides a beautiful vantage point along Old Mill Creek, with views of the boat yard further along.

From the bridge, follow the road right and proceed along as it leads up past an entrance to another boat yard on your right. After a short distance along Lapthorne Lane you will arrive at a fork in the path. Taking the right fork makes for a much more scenic walk and is the way this book will follow. Be warned though, this way does make for an extremely demanding hill climb after passing through Great Copse woodland. Otherwise, you can continue left which takes you up the left-hand side of Hole Copse, onwards passing through several fields.

Ready? Enter into Hole Copse and pass through a wonderful woodland walk that merges into Great Copse. You will catch glimpses of the Old Mill Creek through the tree line. You should even be able to spot the ruins of the circular Hermitage Castle. The stone relic is thought to date from either 1790 or 1890. At low tide, you may even be able to see the sunken hulks and timber skeletons of long abandon boats.

Dartmouth Steam Railway

The Heritage Railway, formally known as the Paignton and Dartmouth Steam Railway, is a railway line running several miles between Paignton and Kingswear located on the eastern shore, opposite Dartmouth.

The line originally opened in 1859. During the Beeching cuts of the 1960s, the Paignton to Kingswear line met its end, closing in 1972. It was then sold to Dart Valley Light Railway Ltd where it then operated as a seasonal service.

This line, as mentioned previously in the transport section, provides a spectacular route along the coast of Torbay. Unlike other heritage railways, the ine operates as a commercial operation, not relying on charitable donations or volunteers to keep it running.

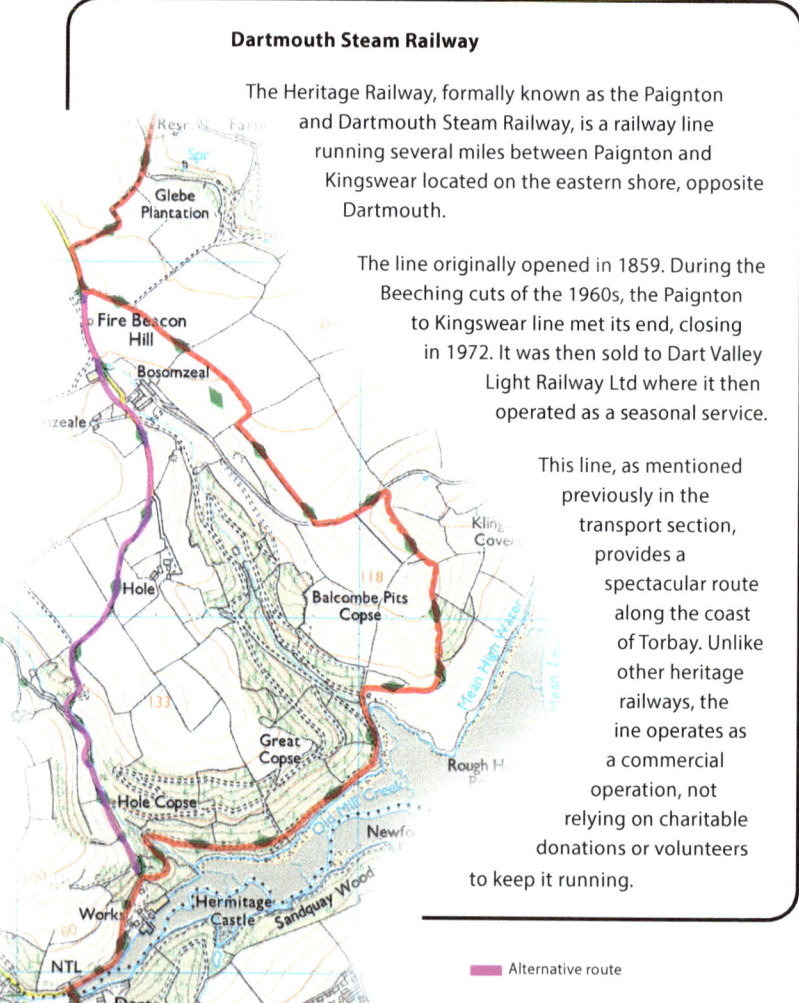

■ Alternative route

Upon leaving Great Copse you will enter out onto a clearing, this point provides fantastic views overlooking the area where Old Mill Creek enters into the River Dart. As you round the corner, it is also the start point of a roughly 500 meter arduous uphill climb, perhaps the most strenuous point of the whole route. There are plenty of opportunities though to take a rest and peer through the trees and take in the scenery of the surrounding valley towards Noss on Dart Marina. If you time it right, you may even see the Dartmouth Steam Railway locomotives thundering along the tracks that run alongside the eastern shore.

Once you have conquered the hill and have reached the top, looking back provides more beautiful views but this time looking down the Dart and towards the Britannia Royal Naval College. As such, this vantage point offers a remarkable view of the historic building. Next, continue along the track and follow the signs. You will pass through several other fields before entering out onto a country lane at Fire Beacon Hill. Proceed down a short distance and enter right into a field and proceed down past Glebe Plantation. You will join up with another footpath that runs horizontally across. Here, turn right and follow the remainder of the track down into Lower Dittisham.

Alternative route

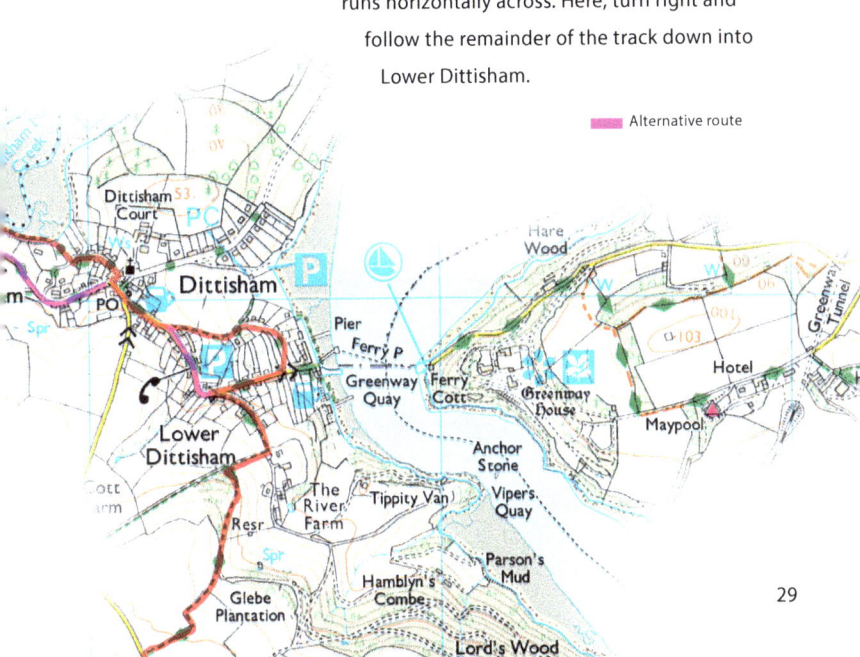

LEG 2 - DITTISHAM TO TUCKENHAY

Dittisham Harbour

Dittisham

OS Grid Ref: SX 863 547
District: South Hams
OS Explorer map: OL20 South Devon

Leg Distance: 6.6 km / 4.1 miles
Elevation Gain: 180 m

Points of interest

Dittisham Ferry

Greenway House & Garden
(reached via ferry)

St George's Church

Post Office & Stores

Public Car Parking

Accommodation & Eateries

Ferry Boat Inn

Red Lion Inn

Anchor Stone Cafe

Cobwebs Cottage

Bows, Riverside Road

Fingles Luxury Country House B&B

Cott Farm B&B

Dittisham, with a population of roughly 420 residents, is the first settlement you will come across on the route. Located on the banks of the River Dart, it is approximately two miles upstream from Dartmouth.

This unspoilt village provides a beautiful, relaxing, riverside escape. It is home to a number of local stores, a post office, and a few pubs: the Red Lion, the Ferry Boat Inn, and the Anchor Stone Cafe. The most notable feature of the village is St George's Church - situated in Dittisham for more than a thousand years.

Lower Dittisham also offers a short ferry trip across to visit Greenway House. Now owned by the National Trust, Greenway House was once home to the famous crime novelist, Agatha Christie. The crossing point is also located next to the Ferry Boat Inn, a pub that offers a beautiful riverside seating area if you are feeling thirsty.

At the time of writing, ferries run daily through the summer but only at weekends during winter. More information on timings and prices can be found by visiting the following link: **www.dittishamferries.co.uk.**

Greenway Estate

Located on the eastern shore of the River Dart, Greenway House is notable for being home of the famed detective novel writer, Agatha Christie.

Although in the late sixteenth century a Tudor mansion called Greenway Court stood on the grounds, the present Georgian building is likely to have been built towards the end of the eighteenth century. Agatha Christie bought the estate with her husband in 1938 and lived there until their respective deaths in 1976 and 1978. The house features under various guises in several of her works.

The grade II listed house and its surrounding gardens contain plants from the southern hemisphere. Since its acquisition by the National Trust in 2000, these plants can now be viewed by the public.

■ Alternative route

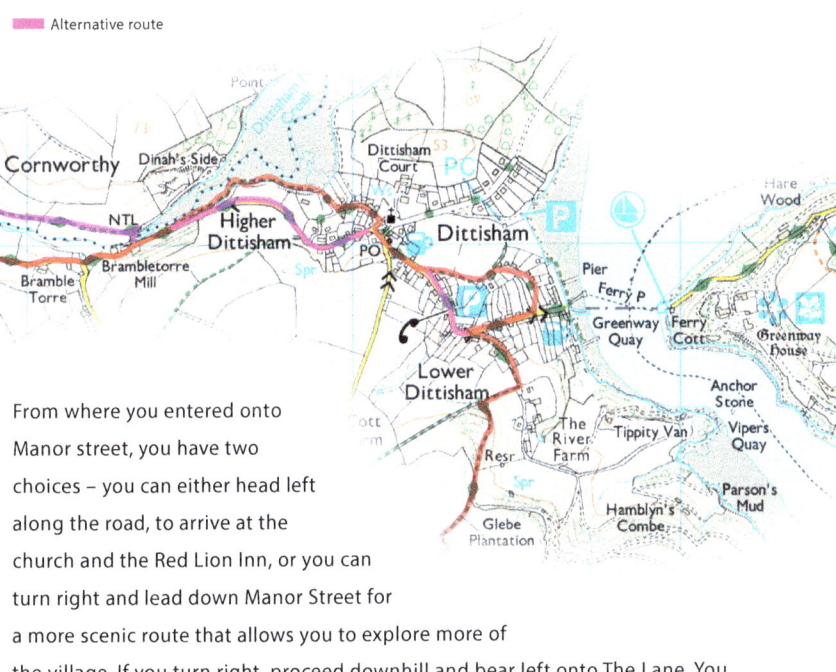

From where you entered onto Manor street, you have two choices – you can either head left along the road, to arrive at the church and the Red Lion Inn, or you can turn right and lead down Manor Street for a more scenic route that allows you to explore more of the village. If you turn right, proceed downhill and bear left onto The Lane. You can reach the pedestrian ferry crossing by continuing down to the bottom of the hill. Following the road around to the left, you will pass a number of beautiful stone cottages.

The path then leads up around the perimeter of the large field to your right. A bench can be found half way up. It provides a great spot for some rest with views looking down towards the Dart. Once you reach the top of the hill enter out onto The Lane, where you will pick up the main route again. From here continue along the road until you arrive at The Red Lion Inn.

Upon reaching St George's Church, you will be faced again with the possibility of another two routes. You can either continue along the road named Higher street, or, if the river is at low tide, you can enjoy a short walk along the shore of the estuary.

Looking across the River Dart

To take the latter small diversion, take a right at the front of St George's Church onto Lower Street and follow the road down until the slipway on your left as it leads down to the river's edge. Upon entering the river bank, follow the shore line around to the left. Take care as there is an abundance of seaweed and slippery mud. Continue around until you join back up with the road and arrive at Brambletorre Mill.

Alternative route

Join the road and proceed straight. Take the next right and continue straight until you come to a road leading off on your right. Follow the sign for Finglas Country House. Continue along the road, bypassing the hotel. Once at the bend, continue straight up the narrow gravel track and take the first right after a few metres. Here, the trail then leads upwards to Broadgates, another fairly steep incline. Keep a look out for an abandoned house on your right when ascending. At the top, you should then descend into the south-eastern side of the village of Cornworthy. Bypass St Peter's Church and pass through the centre of the village; you can find the Madruth Inn on your right.

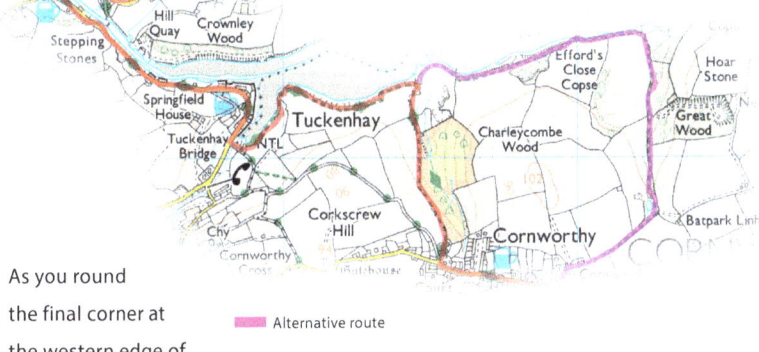

As you round the final corner at the western edge of

▰ Alternative route

the village, keep right and proceed to the right of the houses that lead up Hothill Lane. Enter into the field and follow the path down to Harbourne River, another river that feeds into the River Dart. Lead left and follow along the raised bank to be brought out into Tuckenhay, the next settlement.

Leading towards Tuckenhay

LEG 3 - TUCKENHAY TO TOTNES

The Maltsters Arms, Tuckenhay

Tuckenhay

OS Grid Ref: SX 818 560
District: South Hams
OS Explorer map: OL20 South Devon

Leg Distance: 6.1 km / 3.7 miles
Elevation Gain: 186 m

Accommodation & Eateries

Tuckenhay Mill

Riverside House

The Maltsters Arms

The Hunters Lodge Inn

2 Mill Cottages

Tuckenhay is 2.5 miles south of Totnes and is the final settlement before reaching the town. The hamlet is situated on the bank of Bow Creek, on the estuary of the Harbourne River - another river that flows into the River Dart.

The name Tuckenhay can be traced back to 1550 where it is first recorded. It has an industrious past as a papermill, producing high-grade handmade paper, opened in 1829 and operated up until the late twentieth century. The area now, however, operates largely as a luxury holiday accommodation destination.

Down at the quay, you will find the pub/restaurant The Maltsters Arms, once owned by the British celebrity chef, Keith Floyd.

To continue with the trail, lead off past The Maltsters Arms bypassing it on your right. Keeping to the road, continue straight. If the river is low, keep a lookout for the stepping stones on your right as this presents a handy shortcut. Otherwise, you can continue along the road where you will find another pub named the Waterman's Arms, another great place with a beautiful outdoor seating area that offers a refreshing drink and pause. Cross over the bridge and follow the road around to the right ensuring you keep to the road. The first right is where you would arrive out if you crossed the river using the stepping stones.

Follow the road around to the left and continue uphill passing through the picturesque village of Ashprington. Here, you will pass yet another pub named The Durant Arms, located in the centre of the village. Dominating the skyline is St David's Church.

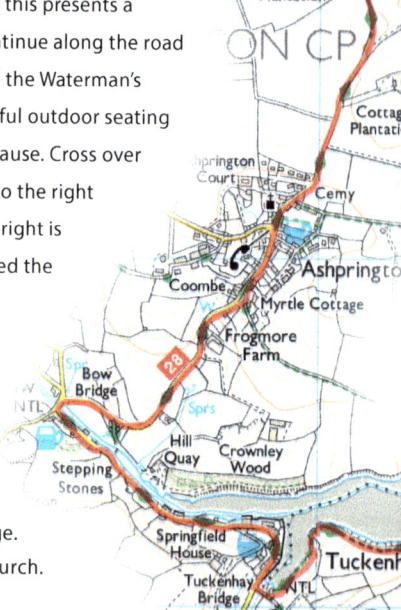

Once past the church, keep heading straight ahead uphill. This road leads up to Sharpham House, a 550-acre estate with award winning cheese and wine. Upon arrival at the pillars that lead onto the estate, enter through the walkway situated to the left. Here, the route leads down in-between a number of fields and Lower Gribble Plantation.

After the plantation, enter into the field on your right. This vantage point provides a panoramic view of the River Dart and across the valley beyond. If visibility is good, you will even be able to see Haytor in the far off distance, one of Dartmoor's most popular tourist hot spots. Head down into the field to join the track at the bottom. Turn left and proceed along the track. At the end, turn right onto a narrower track. Here the trail leads through Linhay Plantation then over the undulating hill side until the path joins up close to the section of the river named Home Reach, the final stretch before the river enters Totnes. From here, the trail leads through a final patch of woodland. Once through it, you will enter into the southern part of Totnes and see a large boatyard down to your right.

Just before the end of the boat yard, proceed up the zig-zagged path to your left and follow the lane down through into the southern residential area. Upon entering through the gate and joining the road, turn right and head down to the Steam Packet Inn. Turn left onto New Walk and continue along this road for 300m to the roundabout and to the start of Fore Street. Fore Street is the main road that leads up through Totnes town centre; at the very top, you can find Totnes Castle.

FINISHING AT TOTNES

Fore Street, Totnes

Totnes

OS Grid Ref: SX 805 603
District: South Hams
OS Explorer map: OL20 South Devon

Points of interest
Totnes Castle
Dartington Hall (Approx 2.9 m)
Totnes Museum
The Time House Art Museum
Leachwell Spring
Fashion and Textiles Museum
Rare Breeds Farm
South Devon Railway
Train Station
Public Car parking

Accommodation & Eateries
The Dartmouth Inn
Waterside Bistro in Devon
King William IV
The Albert Inn
Steam Packet Inn
The Old Forge at Totnes
Four Seasons Guest House

Buses
Gold - Plymouth to Torquay via Totnes
X64 - Exeter to Dartmouth via Totnes
100 - Totnes to Paignton
177 - Totnes to Newton Abbot

The ancient market town of Totnes sits at the head of the estuary of the River Dart. It lies within the area of South Devon designated by the government as an Area of Outstanding Natural Beauty.

The name of the town has a legendary tale associated with it. According to the History of the Kings of Britain, originally written by Geoffery of Monmouth around 1136, Totnes was the town from where the mythical founder, Brutas of Troy, a descendant of the Trojan hero Aeneas, first came ashore to Britain and proclaimed the town to be called Totnes. The supposed stone where he first stepped foot is set into the pavement of Fore Street, marked with the inscription 'Brutus Stone' above it.

However, despite the fabled tale, the first validated account of Totnes can be traced back to when the first castle was built in 907; it occupies a position on a large hill above the town.

The town acquired market town status by the twelve century and became the second richest town in Devon by 1523. With its position along one of the main roads that leads through Devon, and its closeness to the easily navigable river Dart, the town flourished. Evidence of this can be found in the number of merchants' houses built during the sixteenth and seventeenth centuries present in the town. It is said to even have more listed buildings than any other town in the country.

In more recent times, namely 2006, the town became one of the first 'Transition towns'. This model was based on promoting self-sufficiency and reducing the effects on the environment and climate destruction. Today, it has a notable New Age community; the town provides a thriving centre for art, music, and theatre. There are a multitude of great local amenities to be found off Fore Street. The main road that leads from the castle down to the riverside is littered with small independent retailers and unique shops that promote fair trade and offer ethical products.

Totnes Castle

Sitting atop a large hill above the town, the remains of the surviving stone keep, dating from the fourth century, is perhaps one of the best preserved examples of a motte-and-baily castle in the whole of England.

It is largely believed that the first castle to appear on the site was built by Juhel of Totnes, one of the leaders of the Breton forces, a lieutenant of William the Conqueror. The feudal barony of Totnes was subsequently granted to him after the invasion in 1068.

The castle later came into custody of William de Barose. By 1326, the keep had fallen into disrepute. A royal order was later passed for its repair and so it was refortified using Devonian limestone and red sandstone. Later, following the war of the roses between 1455 and 1487, the castle again became dilapidated.

Today, the grade II listed castle is under the ownership of English Heritage.

Totnes Castle

USEFUL INFORMATION

ORGANISATIONS

Youth Hostel Association
Web: www.yha.org.uk
Facebook: @WeAreYHA
Twitter: @yhaofficial
Phone: +44 (0) 800 0191700
Email: customerservices@yha.org.uk

Visit Devon
Web: www.visitdevon.co.uk
Facebook: @VisitDevon
Twitter: @VisitDevon

South Hams District Council
Web: www.southhams.gov.uk
Facebook: @southhamsdistrictcouncil
Twitter: @SouthHams_DC
Phone: 01803 861234

English Heritage
Web: www.english-heritage.org.uk
Facebook: @englishheritage
Twitter: @EnglishHeritage
Phone: 0370 333 1181
Email: customers@english-heritage.org.uk

National Trust
Web: www.nationaltrust.org.uk
Facebook: @nationaltrust
Twitter: @nationaltrust
Phone: 0344 800 1895
Email: enquiries@nationaltrust.org.uk

Ramblers
Web: www.ramblers.org.uk
Facebook: @ramblers
Twitter: @RamblersGB
Phone: 020 7339 8500
Email: ramblers@ramblers.org.uk

Dartmouth Visitors Centre
Web: www.discoverdartmouth.com
Facebook: @discoverdart
Twitter: @discoverdart
Phone: 01803 834224
Email: holidays@discoverdartmouth.com

Long Distance Walkers Association
Web: www.ldwa.org.uk

COMMUNITY INFORMATION

Dartmouth
Web: www.dartmouth.org.uk

Dittisham
Web: www.dittisham.org.uk

Cornworthy
Web: www.cornworthy.com/cms/

Ashprington & Tuckenhay
Web: www.ashpringtonandtuckenhay.co.uk

Totnes
Web: www.visittotnes.co.uk

PUBLIC TRANSPORTATION

National Rail Enquiries
Web: www.nationalrail.co.uk
Phone: 03457 48 49 50

National Express
Web: www.nationalexpress.com/en
Phone: 0871 781 8181

First Bus
Web: www.firstgroup.com/somerset
Phone: 0345 602 0121

Interactive Devon bus routes
Web: www.traveldevon.info/bus/interactive-bus-map/

Traveline
Web: www.traveline.info
Phone: 0871 200 2233

Stagecoach
Web: www.stagecoachbus.com
Email: southwest.enquiries@stagecoachbus.com
Phone: 01392 42 77 11

Dartmouth Steam Railway
Web: www.dartmouthrailriver.co.uk
Email: bookings@dsrrb.co.uk
Phone: 01803 555872

Greenway Ferry
Web: www.greenwayferry.co.uk
Email: info@greenwayferry.co.uk
PhoneL 01803 882 811

SELECTED EATERIES

Dartmouth

Dartmouth Arms
Web: www.thedartmoutharms.com
Phone: 020 8488 3117
Email: dartmouth@innpublic.com

George & Dragon
Web: www.gandddartmouth.co.uk
Phone: 01803 832325
Email: gandddartmouth@gmail.com

The Floating Bridge
Web: www.thefloatingbridge.co.uk
Phone: 01803 832354
Email: info@thefloatingbridge.co.uk

The Ship in Dock Inn
Web: www.theshipindockinn.co.uk
Phone: 01803 839614
Email: info@theshipindockinn.co.uk

Wheelhouse
Web: www.wheelhousedartmouth.co.uk
Phone: 01803 834446

Café Alf Resco
Web: www.cafealfresco.co.uk
Phone: 01803 835880
Email: info@cafealfresco.co.uk

Rockfish Takeaway
Web: www.therockfish.co.uk
Phone: 01803 832800

The Cherub Inn
Web: www.the-cherub.co.uk
Phone: 01803 832571
Email: info@the-cherub.co.uk

Dittisham

Ferry Boat Inn
Web: www.ferryboatinndittisham.pub
Phone: 01803 722 368
Email: simonfbi@hotmail.co.uk

Red Lion Inn
Web: www.redliondittisham.co.uk
Phone: 01803 722235
Email: enquiries@redliondittisham.co.uk

Anchor Stone Café
Web: www.anchorstonecafe.co.uk
Phone: 018037 22365
Email: info@anchorstonecafe.co.uk

Totnes

The Dartmouth Inn
Web: www.dartmouthinntotnes.co.uk
Phone: 01803 863252
Email: thedartmouthinn.totnes@gmail.com

Waterside Bistro Totnes
Web: www.watersidebistro.com
Phone: 01803 864069
Email: restaurant@watersidebistro.com

King William IV
Web: www.kingwilliamtotnes.co.uk
Phone: 01803 866689
Email: kingwilliamtotnespub@gmail.com

Steam Packet Inn
Web: www.steampacketinn.co.uk
Phone: 01803 863880
Email: steampacket@buccaneer.co.uk

SELECTED ACCOMMODATION

Dartmouth

Royal Castle Hotel
Web: www.royalcastle.co.uk
Phone: 01803 833033
Email: enquiry@royalcastle.co.uk

Browns Hotel
Web: www.brownshoteldartmouth.co.uk
Phone: 01803 832572
Email: enquiries@brownshoteldartmouth.co.uk

Dittisham

Cobwebs Cottage
Web: www.cobwebscottage.co.uk
Phone: 01803 722246

Fingles Luxury Country House B&B
Web: www.fingals.co.uk
Phone: 01803 722398
Email: info@fingals.co.uk

Cott Farm B&B
Web: www.cottfarmdittisham.co.uk
Phone: 01803 722249
Email: doreen@cottfarmdittisham.co.uk

Tuckenhay

Tuckenhay Mill
Web: www.tuckenhaymill.co.uk
Phone: 01803 732624
Email: enquiries@tuckenhaymill.co.uk

Riverside House
Web: www.riverside-house.co.uk
Phone: 01803 732837
Email: felicity.riverside@hotmail.co.uk

The Maltsters Arms
Web: www.tuckenhay.com
Phone: 01803 732350
Email: bookings@tuckenhay.com

Totnes

The Old Forge at Totnes
Web: www.oldforgetotnes.com
Phone: 01803 862174
Email: enquiries@oldforgetotnes.com

Four Seasons Guest House
Web: www.fourseasonstotnes.com
Phone: 01803 862146
Email: info@fourseasonstotnes.co.uk

TAXIS

Dartmouth

Devon Taxis
Phone: 01803 833778

Mickys Taxis
Phone: 07812 088935

Bluebird Taxis
Phone: 070 9330 3074

Kestrel Taxis
Phone: 01803 832526

Totnes

Dart Taxis
Phone: 01803 865575

Taxis Totnes - Fox Family Cars
Phone: 07930 371427

Abacus Cabs
Phone: 07790 345321

Eagle Cabs
Phone: 07412 841214

ADDITIONAL INFO

Dartmouth Castle
Web: www.english-heritage.org.uk/visit/places/dartmouth-castle/

Bayard's Cove Fort
Web: www.english-heritage.org.uk/visit/places/bayards-cove-fort/

Dart Mouth Higher Ferry
Web: www.dartmouthhigherferry.com
Phone: 078665 31687

Dart Harbour & Navigation Authority
Web: www.dartharbour.org
Phone: 01803 832337
Email: info@dartharbour.org

South Devon Railway
Web: www.southdevonrailway.co.uk
Phone: 01364 644 370
Email: trains@southdevonrailway.org

Greenway Gardens
Web: www.nationaltrust.org.uk/greenway
Phone: 01803842382
Email: greenway@nationaltrust.org.uk

Dartmouth Museum
Web: www.dartmouthmuseum.org
Phone: 01803 832923
Email: dartmouth@devonmuseums.net

Greenway Ferry Service & Pleasure Cruises
Web: www.greenwayferry.co.uk
Phone: 01803 882 811
Email: info@greenwayferry.co.uk

Dittisham Ferries
Web: www.dittishamferries.co.uk
Phone: 07907 528 201
Email: dittishamferries@gmail.com

Totnes Castle
Web: www.english-heritage.org.uk/visit/places/totnes-castle/

Totnes Museum
Web: www.totnesmuseum.org
Phone: 01803 863821
Email: info@totnesmuseum.org

Dartington Hall
Web: www.dartington.org
Phone: 01803 847000
Email: info@dartington.org

EMERGENCY SERVICES

Dartmoor Search and Rescue
If it is an emergency, dial 999 and ask for police.
Web: www.dsrtashburton.org.uk
Facebook: www.facebook.com/dartmoorrescueashburton
Twitter: @Dartmoor_SRTA
Email: info@ndsart.org.uk

RNLI Dart
If it is an emergency, dial 999 and ask for Coastguard.
Web: www.dartlifeboat.org.uk
Facebook: @dartrnlilifeboat
Twitter: @dartrnli
Phone: 01803 839224

NOTES:

NOTES:

www.ingramcontent.com/pod-product-compliance
Lightning Source LLC
Chambersburg PA
CBHW061805070526
44586CB00023B/2720